FLIP SIDES

Should We Drill for Oil in Protected Areas?

YES!

Jessica Harwood

MONDO

Contents

Oil in Our Lives

Look around you. You may not realize it, but you are surrounded by oil. Oil can power your car, refrigerator, computer, and anything else that uses electricity. Oil might also heat your home. Oil and its products provide more than 60 percent of the energy used in the United States of America.

Plastic, which is used to make thousands of products, is produced from oil. Oil is also used to make crayons, lip balm, tires, and fleece fabrics. Oil even helps provide us with food, since farmers use pesticides and fertilizers made from oil to grow crops. With so many people around the world depending on oil for energy and for the products they need, how can we make sure we will continue to have enough?

This book looks at how we use oil today and whether we should pursue oil use and exploration in the future. Because oil is a nonrenewable resource, once it is used up there will be no more left. People disagree, however, about how much oil we have left and how long it will last. Should we, therefore, continue to use oil and drill for more, even in protected areas? Or should we start to use less and look for other sources of energy?

Some people believe that oil is essential in our lives and that we should do whatever we can to find more of it. Others believe that since oil is running out, we should use less of it and look for alternative resources.

As you read this book, think about the arguments for continuing oil exploration and the arguments against it. Try to understand the different points of view, and then decide which solution you think is best.

In this part of the book, you will read the viewpoint of Theodore D. Petro, someone who believes we should continue to use oil as we have in the past and do whatever we can to locate more domestic oil (oil from our own country). Before you read Theodore's arguments, however, you need some basic information. Turn to the pages bordered in blue in the center of this book for some background on oil. Then turn back to page 5 for Theodore's views on the issue.

Introduction

Meet Theodore D. Petro, who is pro oil-drilling

My name is Theodore D. Petro. I am the owner of a plant that makes plastic wrap—everything from bubble wrap to the covering on CD cases. All of the products we manufacture are made from oil. But that is not all we use oil for. We use oil for energy to run all of our machines and to light the factory. We use oil in the form of gasoline and jet fuel to power the trucks and planes that bring our products to people across the United States and the world. My company could not exist if it were not for oil.

Oil is necessary for the survival of my business, for the well-being of my workers, and for the production of the plastic packaging for products that you use every day. But mine is just one small company. There are many other factories the same size or larger that also depend on oil.

I believe that we need to do whatever we can to make sure that oil remains both plentiful and affordable. We need enough oil to continue creating the products that Americans use, to provide jobs for people, and to transport people and products. Without oil our lives would be very different and much more difficult.

Lately I have been worried that we might be on the brink of another energy crisis. There are problems in the Middle East, and our government is trying to keep the oil there safe so that the supply is not interrupted. Maybe you have noticed that the cost of gasoline has gone up quite a lot—just ask your parents. Not only does it cost more to run my trucks, but all of the oil that we use is more expensive. My company has actually been losing money, and I have had to lay off some workers. I am worried about what will happen to my business and others like it if oil prices keep rising.

The oil industry is the source of a lot of jobs and income throughout the world. It employs about 1.4 million workers, and almost four times that many work in jobs that are related to the oil industry. If the oil industry collapses, many people could lose their jobs.

Nearly everyone depends on oil in some way. What will happen to people who drive cars if the oil supply is stopped? How will people get to work? How will kids get to school? How will food get to the grocery store? Like many people, every day I drink out of a plastic cup, wear fabrics made from plastic, and use products wrapped in plastic packaging. Obviously something must be done to make sure that oil is affordable and available so that we can continue to live our lives as we are accustomed.

I believe we must search for oil in all possible places. We should use our knowledge and technology to extract any and all oil that we can, particularly within the United States' borders. Oil found here will help the United States economy. If we drill for more oil in the United States, we will be able to control the oil ourselves and provide more jobs. In the following pages, I am going to explain why I believe oil is so important to the United States and why we should drill for oil even in protected areas.

Predictions of peak oil have been wrong in the past. Why should we believe them now?

The concept of peak oil is only a theory; it has not been proven. It is based on the idea that there is a fixed amount of oil on Earth and that it will soon be used up. However, over the years, people in the oil industry have regularly discovered new sources of oil and new ways of finding and extracting it, and there is no reason to believe they won't continue to do so. For example, in the 1970s during the energy crisis, oil companies managed to find new sources of oil in England, Norway, and Mexico. Surely there is oil to be found in other new places as well.

We already have powerful computers and seismic equipment that help produce images of rock layers below the ground and make it much easier to find new oil. Oil companies can drill horizontally and tap several oil deposits at once to obtain more oil. Geologists have even figured out how to get oil from rock called oil shale and from oil sands. Scientists have found many new ways to locate and extract oil, so it is unlikely that we will run out.

In fact, people who talk about peak oil have been proven wrong several times already. First they predicted that we would reach peak oil in the 1970s, then in 1995, and then in 2000. Some say that we will reach it any day now. Well, so far their predictions have not been correct. How can we believe in an idea that has been proven wrong at least three times?

Geologists say they cannot know for sure where they will find oil next. We do not know how much oil hides beneath the ground, and therefore we cannot possibly know when we are running out. What we do know, however, is that oil is essential to our lives.

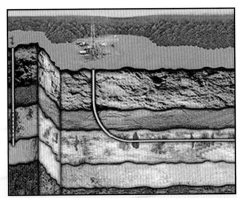

Horizontal drilling

We should not depend on the Middle East for oil. We need to find new, safer sources.

We use oil every day in almost everything we do; it is vital to our lives. But less than half of that oil comes from our own country. In other words, we import about 60 percent of our oil, much of which comes from the Middle East. In 2005 the United States imported more than 500,000 barrels of oil per day from Iraq alone. Yet many countries in the Middle East are not friends of the United States.

On September 11, 2001, terrorists from the Middle East attacked the United States. The United States government is working hard to decrease the threat of terrorism, yet we continue to depend for our oil on countries that support terrorists. We shouldn't depend on an area of the world that poses a threat to our safety. Besides, the Middle East is not a reliable source of oil, as we discovered during the Yom Kippur War of 1973. The oil in the Middle East might run out in the future, or governments there might decide to stop exporting oil to the United States. Therefore, we need to obtain oil from safe and secure sources instead.

The best way to ensure the safety and security of our oil supply is through independence: We need to produce our own oil. We already have found a lot of oil in California, the Rocky Mountains, and Alaska—so why aren't we extracting it? It makes sense to use our own natural resources as we need them. In the face of another possible energy crisis, where we can't get enough oil from present sources, we should find a solution that allows us to continue to live as we always have. Using domestic oil is a cheap, easy, and safe way for us to get the oil that our country needs.

New technology allows us to drill for oil without ruining the land, and current drilling in Alaska has not had a serious impact on wildlife.

Burning oil is one of the cleanest ways to produce electricity. Oil does not create as much air pollution when it is burned as coal or wood does. Nuclear energy leaves waste that can be dangerous and even deadly to humans. If the goal is to have a clean, healthy environment, we should use oil for energy because it leaves less air and land pollution.

Environmental groups argue that drilling for oil is harmful to the land, but oil companies work hard to do as little damage as possible. The Nature Conservancy, an environmental organization, states that "careful drilling can coexist with environmental protection." The group even says that careful oil drilling can actually contribute to protecting the environment. For example, some oil companies have donated land to environmental groups such as the Nature Conservancy. By doing this, the oil-producing lands become protected in addition to being used for our needs.

The Arctic National Wildlife Refuge (ANWR) is a great example of how concerned our nation is about protecting the environment while still being able to drill for oil. Most geologists agree that billions of barrels of oil could be recovered from this area in Alaska, and the United States government has promised not to ruin the environment while doing so. President George W. Bush said, "I campaigned hard on the notion of having environmentally sensitive exploration at ANWR." Also, since many legislators are concerned about the effect oil drilling will have on ANWR, they will work hard to ensure that safeguards are in place before giving their approval to drill there. Any drilling that ends up taking place in Alaska will be done very carefully.

Before beginning to drill, scientists plan to research the habitats of the animals that live there in order to protect them. Pipelines will be

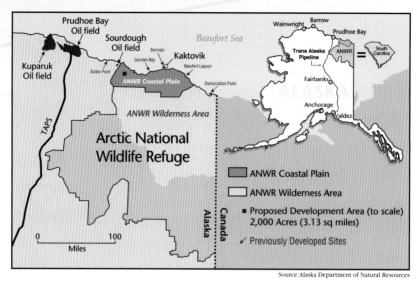

Source: Alaska Department of Natural Resources

constructed above ground so that animals will be able to go beneath them. Because gravel isn't natural to the arctic environment, oil companies instead will create roads of ice on which to drive their vehicles. The oil companies have obviously thought carefully about ways to keep from harming this habitat. In addition, the government has promised that $1 billion from oil drilling profits in Alaska will go to land conservation projects across the United States.

New oil-drilling technology now enables more oil to be extracted from the earth while causing less harm to the environment. For example, powerful computers and seismic equipment enable the oil companies to drill fewer wells while searching for oil. Only about one fifth as many exploratory wells are drilled now compared to in the past. Therefore there is less impact on the land.

In addition, the oil wells themselves now have less impact on the environment. This is because the wells can now be drilled horizontally underground. Instead of drilling many vertical holes to get at the oil beneath the surface, they can reach as much oil by drilling just one long horizontal hole (see p. 7).

Oil companies have also begun to use lighter oil rigs that do not need to be transported on permanent roads. Therefore, temporary roads that will not permanently change the land can be constructed instead. In Alaska the lighter oil rigs can travel over temporary ice roads.

Oil can also now be transported in a way that has less impact on the land. Pipelines that carry the oil from the wells can be placed above ground, causing less damage to plants and animal habitats. The United States government has already built successful raised pipelines in Alaska, including the Trans Alaska Pipeline System, which runs about 800 miles (1,287 km) through Alaska.

If you look at Prudhoe Bay in Alaska, where drilling has been going on since 1977, you see careful, safe extraction of oil. Many Native Americans from the area worked with the oil companies to create the environmental standards, which are among the strictest in the world.

Scientists have studied Prudhoe Bay to see how drilling has affected the animals there, and they found that animal populations have changed little. One of the most important animals in this area is the caribou, a member of the deer family. Caribou move around a lot, and many people worried about what would happen to them as a result of oil drilling.

So far the caribou do not appear to have suffered from the drilling. According to Senator Bob Bennett of Utah, "The caribou herds are bigger [in Prudhoe Bay] now than they were when the pipeline was built." Caribou seem to have learned to protect themselves from the drilling.

These caribou do not seem affected by the pipeline above them.

Drilling for domestic oil will put more money into our economy, create more jobs, and benefit Native Americans in Alaska.

Producing more domestic oil would keep more money in the United States' economy instead of sending money overseas to buy oil. This would benefit the American people because oil would be cheaper. Imported oil is so expensive because OPEC and the other countries that sell it mostly control the price. After OPEC was formed, the price of a barrel of oil went from about $1.90 in 1972 to more than $60 in 2005!

When we import oil, we are forced to pay whatever the exporter asks. In 1979 we paid $60 billion for oil, but in 1981, even though we imported less oil, we paid $80 billion because the price per barrel had gone up so much. In 2005 our foreign oil bill was more than $100 billion. If we produced our own oil, we would not have to pay all this money to foreign governments. Also, natural gas, another important fuel source, is often found along with oil, so if we got more oil from our own land, we could export oil *and* natural gas and make even more money.

For example, if we were to drill for oil in the Arctic National Wildlife Refuge, it is estimated that the United States would save $485 million per day by not buying oil from other countries. In addition to saving all that money, we would actually be able to earn at least $275 million per day from exporting oil. Once people realize how much money can be made from this one oil site, they will surely want to explore other sites as well.

Each state with oil drilling sites would benefit enormously by earning money from the oil produced as well as from oil leases on the land. Drilling in ANWR, for instance, would earn Alaska and the federal government $3.5 billion each over five years just from the oil leases. Alaska would also earn money as the oil is sold—perhaps several million dollars per year.

In addition to state governments making money, oil drilling projects would bring many new jobs to the state. This would help the state's residents, as would the money they could make from leasing their land.

Small businesses that depend on oil for power and raw materials would also benefit from drilling for oil in the United States. Many businesses have had to lay off workers due to rising energy costs, but with cheaper oil they may grow and flourish and hire more employees.

Drilling for oil in the United States would provide more jobs in other industries, too. There would be jobs for geologists to locate the oil, and jobs for workers to extract the crude oil from the ground and refine it. Other people would be needed to produce the many products made from oil. Overall, drilling for oil in the United States would provide as many as 735,000 new jobs.

Drilling for oil in ANWR would also help Native Americans. In fact, the Alaska Federation of Natives, which includes more than 120,000 Eskimos, Aleuts, Inupiat, and other native peoples, has voted in support of drilling on their own land in the Arctic National Wildlife Refuge because they realize how much they have to gain. In the past, some Native-American students from Alaska had to travel as much as 1,000 miles (1,609 km) to go to high school or college. With money that oil drilling would bring to the area, schools could be built in the Native-American students' own neighborhoods. The children living there would be able to get an education while also remaining close to home so they could learn the traditional way of life of their people.

Native-American children living in ANWR

Conclusion

We should drill for oil in protected areas!

You've read a lot of information about why I believe increased domestic oil production is important for the United States. I hope you agree with me that we should pursue more drilling here. When I think about what the future might hold, I am optimistic. In my lifetime I have seen amazing progress in knowledge and technology. Oil allows us to make wonderful products that make our lives better. I hope this progress continues, with new ideas and inventions further improving our standard of living. But this can only happen if we continue to have new supplies of oil.

It is becoming increasingly expensive to buy oil. Much of our oil comes from the Middle East, an unstable area of the world. The Middle East and other countries that produce oil are asking unfairly high prices for their oil. Some people speculate that these countries may actually be running out of oil. So it is important that we look for oil in our own country.

Workers steady a piece of oil-drilling equipment.

There is potentially a lot of oil here, and drilling for it would put more money into the United States' economy in addition to freeing us from a reliance on the Middle East. We should not have to change the way we live because of the high price and limited amount of oil that's available from other countries.

We have the technology and know-how to be safe and careful in our drilling. Our land is important and should be protected, but we cannot ignore the fact that we need the oil that is right here in the United States.

Should We Drill for Oil in Protected Areas?

YES!

All About Oil

What Is Oil and Where Does It Come From?

Oil is a fossil fuel formed from decaying plants and animals. To see how oil is formed, you would have to travel back in time hundreds of millions of years—the earliest oil deposits are actually more than one billion years old. As tiny marine animals and plants (also called plankton) die, they float to the bottom of the ocean, where they are covered with silt and sand. Over millions of years, layers of silt and sand cover layers of plankton, pushing down on them. This pressure, along with the heat from the earth, causes the dead plankton to change into oil. For oil to form, conditions must be perfect over a long period of time, which rarely happens.

Oil exists throughout the world. It's found under sedimentary rock in ancient sea beds, which are places where warm oceans once existed. These warm oceans used to be quite common. In fact it's likely that the ground beneath you is actually layers and layers of dirt that, over many years, have covered an ancient ocean. Oil can be found pretty much anywhere—in inland areas, along the coast, or in the middle of an ocean—as long as there used to be an ancient ocean or lake on that spot.

Sand and silt

Marine animal and plant remains

How oil is formed

1

When oil is found underground, it's trapped in holes in rock—sort of like a hard sponge that's filled with oil. Some deposits cover just a few miles, while others cover hundreds of miles. Some oil deposits, such as the oil sands in Alberta, Canada, are mixed with sand, water, and clay, which makes the oil harder to separate out.

Oil contains a lot of stored energy. When oil is burned, its energy can be changed into other forms of energy, such as electrical or mechanical energy that can be used to power machines. Oil can also be hardened into plastic, and it's easily transported and stored.

The oil that we take out, or extract, from the ground is called petroleum. Liquid petroleum, or crude oil, can range in color from clear to black. It can be thin like water, thicker like honey, or even very thick like tar. The thickest type of oil, called pitch, is almost solid. Liquid petroleum is often found together with natural gas, which can also be used for electricity and heating.

Crude oil is transported in large pipes, called pipelines, or in ships, called oil tankers, to an oil refinery. At the refinery the oil is heated in order to separate it into different forms, including gasoline for cars, liquefied petroleum gas for heating and cooking, fuel oil for heating homes and making electricity, diesel fuel for cars and trucks, and lubricating oil for motors. The residuals, or parts that are left over, can be made into asphalt, tar, plastic, and wax.

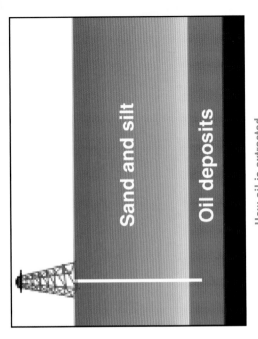

Sand and silt

Oil deposits

How oil is extracted

Crude oil from a well

Early History of Oil

The first people to discover oil lived in Egypt and the Middle East between 5000 and 2000 B.C.E. In these locations, oil was deposited so close to the surface that it came out of the ground on its own in places called seeps. Ancient people found many uses for oil. Oil found on old tools and weapons suggests that ancient Egyptians used it to prevent the weapons from rusting. Archaeologists also have found oil in old buildings and reasoned that it may have been used to glue bricks and tiles together. It appears that the ancient Egyptians also discovered that oil can waterproof things such as boats and clothing. Oil and water do not mix; therefore, anything covered in oil will keep out water. The Egyptians also used oil as a sealant. They put it on mummies to keep the bodies from decaying. They also dabbed oil on wounds to help them heal, because the oil kept out bacteria that could cause infection.

Eventually ancient peoples in various places realized that if they put fire to oil, it would burn for a long time—much longer than wood. With long-lasting oil fires providing heat and light, people could see and continue to work long after the sun went down. Throughout history, people around the world continued to use this miraculous fluid, gradually discovering more and more uses for it.

Hundreds of years ago, in what would become the United States, Native Americans used blankets to skim oil from the surface of water where it had come out of the ground in seeps. They used the oil to waterproof their canoes and as medicine. In fact, during the Revolutionary War (1775–1783), Native Americans showed General George Washington's troops how to treat frostbite by putting oil on their skin.

Ancient Egyptian oil lamp

3

In 1855 an American chemistry professor named Benjamin Silliman, Jr., wrote a report explaining how to distill crude oil to make two important products: lubricants to keep things from sticking and kerosene for fuel. Kerosene was better than whale oil for producing light—it was cheaper; it did not smell as much, and it burned longer. Also, it was easier to make kerosene from crude oil than from coal.

The Oil Rig

As people around the world found different uses for oil, they also began to look for new ways to acquire this useful substance, since there weren't many seeps left. The most common method had been to skim it from lakes and ponds. However, skimming was difficult and did not yield much oil. Then in 1859, Edwin L. Drake, an oil company employee, put together a drilling rig—a machine for drilling down through the earth—and drilled an oil well in Pennsylvania. Drake was lucky enough to find oil not too far beneath the surface. The oil rig made it possible for the first time to get at oil that was trapped underground.

Coal vs. Oil

In the late 1700s and early 1800s in England and other European countries, industries began to burn coal to make steam power to run machines. Coal produced a lot of energy, but it also polluted the air with dirty, black smoke. Americans soon realized that they could use oil to power their machines instead. Oil produced more power, was cheaper than coal, and there was a lot of it around. It also created less pollution and was easy to use.

1859 Drake drilling rig

4

However, coal remained the most popular energy source around the world until the early 1900s. Things began to change in the late 1800s when the United States became the world leader in oil production. Oil-powered machinery enabled American factories to make many products more cheaply than the major industrial countries of Europe where coal was still used. As a result the United States became a leader in world trade.

Soon many countries depended on oil to run their factories and to provide light and other energy. The United States produced about 50 percent of the world's oil until the 1950s. But then the Middle East started discovering huge oil deposits, and things changed.

Oil in the Middle East

In 1908 oil was discovered in Iran. In fact, oil companies soon found that there was a lot of oil in the Middle East. In 1927 oil was discovered in Iraq, and then in Saudi Arabia in 1938. These appeared to be the largest oil deposits on Earth.

As the United States grew, its need for oil increased to beyond what could be obtained domestically. Therefore, many American oil companies quickly bought land and oil rights in the Middle East. By the 1950s major companies—many of which were American—were drilling for oil there. The companies included Exxon, Texaco, Gulf Oil, Mobil, Chevron, Royal Dutch Shell, and British Petroleum (BP), and most are still in business today. These companies controlled much of the oil in the Middle East until 1973.

Not surprisingly, Middle Eastern countries wanted to make more money from the oil found within their borders. In 1960 several countries—Iran, Iraq, Kuwait, Saudi Arabia, and Venezuela—created the Organization of Petroleum Exporting Countries, or

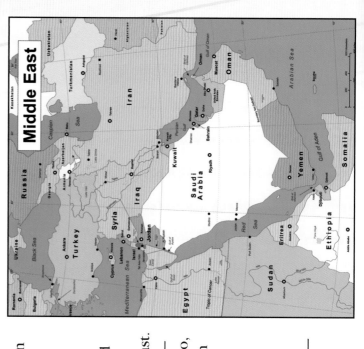

Middle East

OPEC (more countries joined later). These countries, which had about 60 percent of the world's oil reserves within their borders, took control of their oil industries in the 1970s. Since the United States was not in OPEC, it became more difficult and expensive for the United States to get oil.

The Energy Crisis

The changes in the control of oil became more important during the energy crisis of the 1970s. The crisis began in 1973 when war broke out between Arabs and Israelis. The Yom Kippur War led OPEC to raise the price of oil by about 70 percent. Then, to make things worse, the Middle Eastern countries in OPEC became angry at the United States for taking Israel's side in the war. They put the United States under an embargo, which meant they would no longer trade with the United States. Suddenly the United States couldn't import oil from OPEC countries—oil that was needed to sustain Americans' standard of living.

In response to this energy crisis, scientists and engineers in the United States devoted themselves to developing alternative ways of creating energy and making oil-based products. The United States found new sources of oil, as did England, Norway, and Mexico. In 1974 the embargo ended, and OPEC began to trade with the United States again. Today the United States gets most of its oil from Canada, although Mexico, Saudi Arabia, and Venezuela are also important sources.

Finding and Extracting Oil Today

Before oil can be extracted, or removed, from the ground, scientists called petroleum geologists first have to find where oil reserves exist. To do so, the geologists study different rock layers to learn where ancient seas might have been. Often sandy soil marks the spot where an ancient ocean may have been and where oil deposits might exist. To locate oil, geologists also use gravity meters or magnetometers—devices that detect changes in the earth's gravity or magnetism. A decrease in gravity might indicate oil below ground, since oil has less gravitational pull than rock alone. Increases in magnetism can also indicate the presence of oil.

Once geologists have an idea where oil might be, they often use computers and other technology to analyze layers of the earth. They can determine what lies beneath the earth's surface by sending shock waves through the ground and then observing how the waves are reflected back. Because vibrations travel at different speeds through different kinds of rock, the results of such tests help geologists form a picture of the underground layers of the earth and determine whether there might be oil there.

After geologists determine where they think oil might exist, an oil company will drill a test well with a gigantic, powerful drill. But oil companies cannot just go around drilling into the ground wherever they want. Most of the land on Earth is already owned by someone, so oil companies must first get permission to drill. If a company does find oil, it will have to pay the person who owns the land if that land is in the United States. However, in most other major oil-producing countries, the government, and not the individual landowner, owns the right to produce the oil, because that oil is considered a part of the country's natural resources.

If oil is found, the oil company must then pay for an oil lease allowing it to extract the oil. A lease is for a certain period of time and usually specifies the amount of money the owner will get for giving permission to drill, as well as what share of the profits from each barrel of oil produced the owner will receive. The oil company will also study the area to understand how the drilling will impact the environment.

When the oil company is ready to drill, the first step is to clear and flatten the land around where the oil well will be. Oil companies must also build roads leading to the site so that their drilling machines will have easy access. Next they have to make sure that there is water nearby, because a lot of water is needed in the oil-drilling process. If there is no water nearby, they will have to drill a well for water.

Oil companies also need to make sure there's a place to dump all of the rock, dirt, and mud that will have to be removed in order to get to the oil. The companies often create a reserve pit—a large hole lined with plastic—where the waste will go. (Think of it as a giant trash can.) If the drilling is to occur in an area that is environmentally sensitive or fragile, the oil company must completely remove any waste that they create.

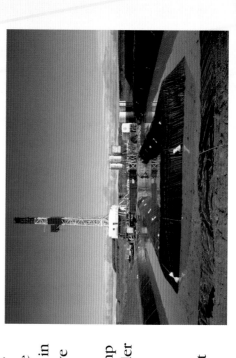

Waste water at oil-drilling site

Oil-drilling rig

Once these preparations have been made, the oil company is finally ready to begin extracting oil. As workers start drilling through layers of rock, they line the walls of the hole with a large pipe or casing to keep the hole from caving in. When the hole is deep enough to reach oil, the oil rig is removed and a pump is put into the pipe. The pump then moves the oil into storage tanks. Oil is measured by the barrel, with one barrel being equal to 42 gallons (large milk jugs) or 159 liters (medium-size soda bottles).

Peak Oil Theory

The theory of peak oil was developed by a Shell oil company geophysicist named Marion King Hubbert in 1956. Realizing that oil is a nonrenewable resource, Hubbert predicted that we will eventually reach a point where less and less oil will be found because we have used up so much. To understand the idea of peak oil, imagine walking up a mountain. As you go higher, you find more and more oil, use it more, and become dependent on it. At the top of the mountain, or the peak, you find the most oil ever. Then as you go down the other side, there is less oil with each step. Unfortunately, just because there is less oil available doesn't mean people use less.

What is even more important about the theory of peak oil is the idea that oil supplies will decrease before our demand for oil decreases, leaving us in a sticky situation. We use more oil today than ever before. Over time we have developed new oil-dependent technologies. There are many more cars on the road than in the past. More plastics are being produced now than even five years ago. After we reach peak oil, we will no longer have enough oil to meet our needs unless new deposits are found or new energy sources are developed.

8

The Problem

No one knows when the earth's supply of oil will run out because no one knows for certain how much is left. What we do know is that people around the world rely on oil for the energy and products they use every day, and that unfortunately there is a limited supply of this resource.

So we find ourselves in a difficult position. Because there is so much uncertainty about how much oil remains, people have different viewpoints on oil use in the future. Both sides look at similar issues to help them to form their opinions, but they arrive at different conclusions. In this book we look at both sides of the following issues:

- Peak Oil—how much oil is left on Earth and when it will run out
- National Security—the safety of the United States as a result of importing oil from unstable countries
- Environmental Impact—how oil affects the environment
- Economics—money matters related to oil

To read the arguments in favor of unlimited use of oil and continued drilling in protected areas, turn to page 5 and read what Theodore D. Petro has to say. To read arguments against the unlimited use of oil and continued drilling in protected areas, turn the book upside down and turn to page 5 of the NO! section to read what Dr. Ann Orne has to say.

Glossary

asphalt
dark substance made from oil residue that is used to pave streets

crude oil
liquid petroleum

diesel fuel
heavy oil, separated from petroleum, used to power diesel engines in cars and trucks

economist
someone who studies how money and products are distributed

ecosystem
community of plants, animals, and microorganisms that are linked by energy and nutrient cycles, and that interact with each other and with the physical environment (a rainforest is an example of an ecosystem)

embargo
forced end to trading with a certain country

energy
power, such as heat and electricity, that is usable

export
to send goods to foreign countries

fossil fuel
energy-producing substance formed from decayed plants and animals that lived long ago

gasoline
mixture of hydrogen and carbon, separated from petroleum, that is primarily used to power engines

global warming
increase in the average temperature of the earth, particularly if it lasts over time

greenhouse gas
gas, such as carbon dioxide or methane, that contributes to potential climate change by trapping the sun's rays around the earth

import
to bring goods in from somewhere else

kerosene
thin oil, separated from petroleum or shale oil, used as a fuel for heating, cooking, and in lamps; also called coal oil or lamp oil

Industrial Revolution
period of time, mainly during the nineteenth century, when major technological and socioeconomic changes took place as a result of steam power and machine manufacturing

liquified petroleum gas
mixture of hydrogen and carbon, separated from petroleum, that is stored as a liquid known as propane or butane; it is primarily used for cooking and heating

lubricating oil
thick oil, separated from petroleum, that is primarily used to prevent sticking

migratory birds
birds that move from one habitat to another due to changes in weather; for example, Arctic terns will migrate from the North Pole to the South Pole in the winter

natural gas
mixture of hydrogen and carbon (in gas form) that is found with petroleum deposits and is used as a fuel

nonrenewable resource
substance existing in nature that cannot easily be replaced once it is used

oil refinery
place where petroleum is separated into various products

oil reserve
known supply of oil found underground

oil rig
structure and machinery that is used to drill an oil well

oil sands
mixtures of sand, water, clay, and a form of oil; the largest of these is found in Alberta, Canada, and is thought to contain 1.7 to 2.5 trillion barrels of oil

oil shale
type of hard rock from which petroleum can be obtained by heating

oil well
hole drilled into the ground from which oil is removed

peak oil
theory that oil production will increase to a certain point and then decline as a result of decreased oil reserves

petroleum
mixture of chemicals called hydrocarbons that is found below the ground in gas, liquid, or solid form; liquid petroleum, or crude oil, is brought to the surface through wells

petroleum geologist
scientist who specializes in looking for and locating oil deposits

plankton
tiny plants and animals that float in the ocean and other bodies of water

sealant
a substance used to seal or protect something

sedimentary rock
rock formed from smaller rocks and other sediment that settles to the bottom of bodies of water

seismic
related to earth vibrations

silt
tiny pieces of soil floating in rivers, ponds, or lakes

water cycle
constant circulation of water among the atmosphere, the land, and the seas

Yom Kippur War
short war (October 6, 1973–October 22, 1973) fought between Israel on one side, and Egypt and Syria with the help of Iraq, Saudi Arabia, and Jordan on the other side; in the end, Israel lost territory

Jessica Harwood

NO!

Should We Drill for Oil in Protected Areas?

FLIP SIDES

Contents

Oil Today and in the Future

Since oil was first discovered, people have found more and more uses for it and become more and more dependent on it. Oil provides power for our cars and appliances, heats our homes, and is used to make many of the products that we take for granted. Yes, oil is very important in our lives, but the fact is that there is not an unending supply of it. Oil is a nonrenewable resource; it takes millions of years to form, so it cannot easily be replaced once it is used up. Therefore should we continue to use as much of this precious resource as we do now? Should we explore protected areas to find new oil supplies? Or should we seek to limit our oil use and find alternatives?

In this book you can read about both sides of the oil issue. Some people believe oil is so important in our lives that we should continue to use it as we have in the past and to drill for it even in protected areas. Others believe that the cost of such action is too high and will cause harm to our environment. They feel that because oil is running out, we need to use less of it and find alternative sources of energy and raw materials for our products.

As you read this book, consider both sides of the issue. Try to understand the arguments that support each viewpoint. Then decide which view of the future of oil makes more sense to you.

In this section of the book, you read the viewpoint of Dr. Ann Orne, someone who believes that we should use less oil and shouldn't pursue further drilling in protected areas of the United States. Before you read Dr. Orne's arguments, however, you should know something about what oil is, its history, and how it became so important in our lives. To do so, turn to the pages bordered in blue in the center of this book. Then read Dr. Orne's side of the issue, which begins on page 5.

Introduction

Meet Dr. Ann Orne, who is anti oil-drilling

My name is Dr. Ann Orne. I am a biologist specializing in migratory birds. I consider myself an environmentalist because I am very concerned about the future of the earth's animals, plants, and natural habitats. I'm concerned about humans, too. I believe that one of the biggest problems facing us right now is our dependence on oil.

The whole world—the United States in particular—depends on oil for energy and for the production of many important products. Yet I am worried that this oil will soon run out. And the price of a barrel of oil goes up almost every day. What will happen if we continue to use more and more oil while the amount of oil that's available decreases?

Much of the oil that we use comes from countries that are unstable and unfriendly to the United States. What if these countries continue to raise the price of oil? What if they should decide to stop selling us their oil altogether? Then what would we do?

As a biologist, I have seen how oil has negatively affected the environment. Drilling for oil often destroys precious plant and animal habitats. I have seen birds lose their homes as a result of oil drilling. When birds migrate, it is very important for them to have places to rest during their long journey, but some of these places have been replaced with oil fields. In addition, waste products from oil drilling and refining can pollute the land and water. Occasionally, the oil itself spills into the water or onto the land when being extracted or transported. This oil can be deadly to birds. When covered in oil, birds lose their ability to fly and stay warm.

When we burn oil, we create air pollution—carbon dioxide and other harmful substances in the atmosphere. Many scientists believe that the gradual increase in carbon dioxide in the atmosphere has actually increased the temperature of the earth, producing what is called global warming. I am worried about what will happen to plants and animals, including humans, as the temperature around them changes.

I believe that we must start using less oil as soon as possible because it is ruining the environment. We should work to develop other forms of energy and other ways to make the products we need. In the process we would create a lot of new jobs, which would be good for the economy.

As you can see, I strongly believe that we should use less oil and not drill for new oil in protected areas. Here's why I feel this way.

Argument One
Peak Oil

We need to reduce the amount of oil we use because supplies are running out.

The peak oil theory says that there is a fixed amount of oil on Earth, and that it will soon be used up. Scientists have proven that 1.3 trillion barrels of oil definitely still exist, and they think there also might be another 500 billion barrels. If there are indeed 1.8 trillion barrels of oil left on Earth, then we should have enough to last until about 2060. This is if we drill everywhere possible, including in protected areas.

Marion King Hubbert predicted that United States oil production would peak in about 1970, which ended up being true. We have not found much oil in the lower 48 states since that time. Luckily it was only the United States that reached peak oil then. We could still get oil from England, Norway, and Mexico, and eventually we began importing oil from the Middle East again. But when oil peaks throughout the world and every country runs out, there will be no new sources of oil to turn to.

The peak oil theory predicts that there will come a time in the future when we won't be able to find enough oil to meet our needs: to power our cars or heat our homes, or to make plastics and other products. The price of oil will go way up, and people might not be able to drive their cars. The cost of anything that's transported in trucks, boats, or planes will increase.

Some people have suggested that we can get oil from tar sands (also called oil sands) and oil shale. However, it requires a lot of energy to take the oil out of the sand, and it's an expensive and time-consuming process. This isn't a good solution.

Since we know that there will be less oil in the future, we should begin to get ready for this to happen. We should reduce the amount of oil we use as soon as possible. It would be easier to gradually reduce our oil consumption now than to deal with a sudden loss of oil later on, which would severely impact our lifestyle and economy.

We should reduce our dependence on oil from the Middle East by using less of it.

Currently the United States uses about 25 percent of the world's oil supply, even though it makes up only about 5 percent of the world's population. We use more oil than any other country. Meanwhile, only about 3 percent of the world's oil supply is found within United States borders. Every year we import about 60 percent of our oil from other countries.

Much of the oil comes from the Middle East, an area where some of the countries are unstable. Recently terrorists in Iraq have targeted oil fields and refineries there because of the United States' presence in that country as well as our reliance on the oil. Our enemies know that they can hurt the United States' economy by stopping the flow of oil on which we so strongly depend.

More than half of our imported oil comes from OPEC countries. It's risky to be so dependent on oil from these countries because whenever OPEC decides to increase the cost of their oil, we would have no choice but to pay it. On the other hand, OPEC countries might decide to save their oil for themselves if they see that it is running out. It doesn't seem wise to continue using so much of a resource that comes from unstable areas.

Some people might argue that to ensure that we have enough oil, we should drill for it right here in the United States. However, the reality is that geologists have not found reliable evidence of much oil here; some estimate that there exists only about a 12-year supply. There is definitely not enough oil to provide the 20 million barrels that Americans use each day.

If the United States used less oil and developed alternative energy sources, we would not need to import the approximately 12 million barrels of oil per day that we currently do. Reducing our oil use would be an easy way to decrease our dependence on other countries. Such independence could help ensure the safety and security of United States citizens.

Environmental Impact

Oil drilling and use can destroy natural habitats and produce water pollution, air pollution, and hazardous waste.

From the beginning, oil exploration and drilling in the United States have caused environmental problems. However, in the 1800s, most people weren't seriously concerned about harming the environment. Instead, they were excited by new inventions, particularly those that would make or save them money. The oil rig was just such an invention. However, people did not stop to think about how extracting oil would affect the land. There were frequent oil spills, and often after a well ran dry, the oil company would simply leave the area without restoring the environment.

Back then, people were less knowledgeable, and they allowed practices that harmed the environment. Today people are more aware that the careless use of resources and technology can severely harm the environment, and they are more likely to do something to stop the destruction.

Habitat Destruction

The process of extracting, transporting, and refining oil can cause an enormous amount of pollution, environmental harm, and change to animal and plant habitats. To find oil, companies sometimes need to drill several holes in one area. Since geologists can't be certain there is oil in a location, workers might drill many test wells and still find nothing at all. And in order to drill these wells, the companies must build roads and bring in all sorts of machinery—all of which can damage the environment.

If companies do find oil after exploratory drilling, the land is then cleared of trees and brush and flattened so the drilling and the building of pipelines can occur. Clearing the land further destroys the habitats of birds, insects, and other animals. Because trees help to hold soil in place, erosion occurs without them as the loosened soil flows off the land

and into the rivers and oceans. In addition, drilling for oil interrupts the natural cycles of the land, such as the water cycle, because water, which is essential to the environment, is stored in the ground.

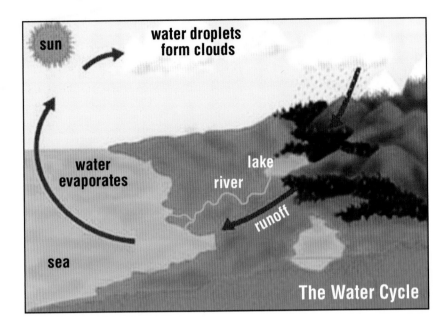

The Water Cycle

Also, in places where oil is more difficult to extract, workers might use explosives to get to the oil. Or they may force a lot of water beneath the earth's surface to flush out the oil. Both of these methods of oil extraction can destroy natural habitats.

Once the oil begins flowing, it must be transported to a refinery in supertankers, barges, trucks, or pipelines. Oil tanker ships are the most common way to transport oil, but pipelines—gigantic above-ground pipes through which the newly extracted oil is transported—are becoming more popular. Every type of transportation creates waste and can result in accidents. In 1994 a pipeline in California broke because of an earthquake and spilled 193,000 gallons of oil into the Santa Clara River.

Today there are actually more miles of oil pipeline than rail lines in the world. Clearing vast amounts of land for these pipelines interferes with natural animal and plant habitats. Also, pipelines are not built to last forever, and old ones run the risk of leaking and polluting an area.

Pollution

When oil companies use water for oil extraction, the water becomes contaminated, or polluted, with chemicals. This waste water is not good for animals and plants, yet some oil companies release the water back into nature.

Salt water that comes from the salt deposits where oil is sometimes found is a waste product of drilling. Oil companies may release this water into local fresh waters even though it is harmful to animals and plants not used to living in a salty habitat. The salt water can also be harmful to humans if it ends up in the drinking water supply.

Oil drilling also leaves behind other hazardous waste, such as the chemicals that are necessary to operate drilling equipment. These chemicals are usually stored in waste pits, and unfortunately sometimes animals mistake the pits for watering holes. Drinking this tainted water can kill them. The chemicals in the waste pits can also seep into towns' drinking water.

Oil spills frequently occur during oil drilling and transportation. The National Academy of Sciences estimates that during the 1990s, some 38,000 tons (34,473 metric tons) of oil were released each year into the oceans due to oil and gas drilling and tanker spills. In addition, gases from the oil drills and other equipment and vehicles cause air pollution. Studies have found that in its lifetime one oil rig can produce as much air pollution as 7,000 cars driving 50 miles (80.5 km) a day.

This penguin is covered in oil from a spill off the coast of South Africa.

11

At the refinery, where crude oil is turned into gas, heating oil, and other products, there can be even more environmental damage. Refineries produce air and water pollution, and solid and hazardous waste. In fact, in 1999 the Environmental Protection Agency (EPA) found that about half of the refineries in the United States had violated the Clean Air Act, which sets standards to prevent air pollution, and about 20 percent had violated the Clean Water Act, which sets rules to prevent water pollution. Water pollution created by refineries has a negative impact on the number and types of fish in an area. People who live near oil refineries also have more cases of respiratory and other illnesses than people who live far from them. Clearly, oil refining does a lot of harm to the environment and to people.

Offshore drilling—where oil rigs extract oil from under the ocean—can be extremely harmful to marine life. Scientists have found that it can destroy seaweed beds, coral reefs, and coastal wetlands. When oil spills into the ocean, it spreads through the water, polluting a large area. In 1998 an offshore oil pipeline in California broke and dumped 21,000 gallons (79,470 l) of oil into the water, damaging a fishing area and killing wildlife. Oil rigs also dump waste products, such as drilling fluid and toxic metal cuttings, into the water.

The Greenhouse Effect

As oil is burned, it releases gases such as carbon dioxide into the air. Carbon dioxide and other gases surround the earth and trap in heat from the sun, like the glass in a greenhouse does. The result, called the greenhouse effect, keeps the earth warm enough for humans to survive. However, some scientists believe that the carbon dioxide from burning oil is making the greenhouse effect stronger.

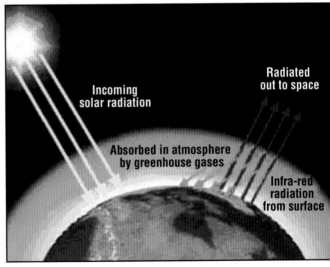

Radiated out to space

Incoming solar radiation

Absorbed in atmosphere by greenhouse gases

Infra-red radiation from surface

How the greenhouse effect happens

Scientists have found that over the past 100 years, the earth's average temperature has increased by about one degree Fahrenheit. During this time people have burned more oil than ever before. The World Energy Council found that from 1990 to 1995 alone, the amount of carbon dioxide released into the air increased by 12 percent. If we continue to burn more oil, thereby producing more carbon dioxide and increasing the greenhouse effect, the earth's temperature will continue to rise. This increase in average temperature is called global warming. Some scientists predict that the global temperature will increase another two to six degrees over the next 100 years. Although the change in temperature may not seem like much, it could have a major negative effect on the environment.

Plants and animals are used to small changes to their habitats, but global warming is causing faster and more dramatic changes. Plants that are used to cold weather may not be able to adjust to warmer temperatures, and they will die out. Some animals may not be able to survive in warmer weather and may be forced to seek out new habitats. Although scientists cannot be certain about what will happen to the environment as a result of warmer temperatures, they know that such changes will be harmful to plants, animals, and even humans.

Global warming is also causing changes to the land itself. Glaciers and icebergs have already begun to melt. As the ice at the North Pole and the South Pole melts, the extra water causes the level of the oceans to rise. Sea levels could rise anywhere from several inches to three feet (.914 m) over the next century, flooding coastal areas. Already, an island in the Pacific Ocean, Tuvalu, is slowly being evacuated because the rising ocean is beginning to flood the land.

Global warming might also cause less rain to fall in some places, causing drought. In some parts of the world, people might not be able to grow the food that they need. Plants and animals will not be able to survive without enough water.

Impacts of Current Drilling Projects in the United States

Some people propose that we look for new sources of oil right here in the United States. Unfortunately, some of our current oil drilling projects are already causing a lot of environmental problems. Protected areas are sections of land where certain activities that might harm native animals and plants are forbidden. These areas are established in order to protect the environment, including plants and animals. By 2002, 7,448 protected areas had been established in the United States, covering approximately 578,000 square miles (1,497,013 sq km)—almost 16 percent of the land. Surprisingly, oil companies are now allowed to drill in some of these protected areas.

One of the areas is the Los Padres National Forest in California. One reason the area is protected is that it is home to 23 threatened or endangered animal species, including the California condor. There are only 44 condors still alive in the wild. A few years ago a condor dipped its head into a pool of oil from a drilling site and then rubbed the oil on a chick; the chick later died. This is the kind of tragedy that will occur more often if more protected areas are opened up to oil drillers.

In addition, the drinking water for the Santa Barbara area drains from this spot, so if an oil spill occurred, the drinking water could get contaminated. Drilling in this protected area has proven harmful to animals, plants, and

California condor

even humans. Geologists' estimates of the amount of oil in this area is only a few days' supply of oil for the United States—84 million barrels. Does this small amount of oil seem worth the environmental risk?

Oil companies have also drilled on protected land in Texas City, Texas, where the endangered Attwater's prairie chicken lives. There are only about 50 birds living in the wild, down from about 456 in 1993. This bird can only survive in certain coastal prairie grasslands, but that has not stopped oil companies from searching for oil in this habitat.

In Prudhoe Bay, Alaska, oil companies have been drilling since 1977 and extract about one million barrels of oil per day. The companies have leases that will allow them to continue drilling for many years. Originally the drilling was meant to take place on just 12,000 acres (48.6 sq km) of land. However, the roads, wells, and exploratory work have left an impact on a whopping 640,000 acres (2,590 sq km)! Not only has the drilling itself damaged the land, but since 1995 there have been an average of 400 spills per year of different substances related to the oil drilling process. Damage can still be seen from spills that occurred almost 30 years ago. Clearly, the oil companies are hurting Alaska's habitats.

A grizzly bear at a dump in the oil fields in Prudhoe Bay, Alaska

The Arctic National Wildlife Refuge (ANWR) is the next protected area that could be destroyed as a result of oil exploration. In 1960 President Dwight D. Eisenhower established ANWR as a protected area. He considered it to be America's last unspoiled frontier and wanted to protect the diversity of plants and animals in this habitat.

Hundreds of plants are able to grow here despite the cold, snow, strong winds, and thin soil. If this habitat is destroyed, these arctic plants will die out. There are also some 230 animal species, including at least 38 different mammal species and more than 150 bird species, that live in ANWR. Among these animals are grizzly bears, moose, musk oxen, wolves, foxes, and polar bears.

One of the animals inhabiting the Arctic National Wildlife Refuge is the caribou, a member of the deer family. Caribou live in immense herds; the herd in Area 1002 of the refuge has about 130,000 caribou. Studies have found that when female caribou are ready to give birth, they usually avoid pipelines and oil fields. This means that the female caribou in Area 1002 will likely abandon this spot if drilling is introduced there and that the yearly birth rate will likely decrease. Additionally, if the caribou are forced to move from this area because of drilling, they may have to move to a place where there is less food—and more predators.

Alaska is also an important place on the migration route of many birds, such as loons and snow geese. Many migratory birds stop to rest in Area 1002, but if there are oil rigs and pipelines around, it will no longer be a very inviting resting place.

Many animal scientists oppose the drilling in this area; however, it's not only animals that will be at risk if we start to drill in ANWR. Several groups of Native Americans live on this land, and drilling could damage their land or even take it away. At risk are both the caribou that they depend on for food and their drinking water; drilling might pollute it or use it up. In many other places, drilling has destroyed native peoples' cultures and traditions as well as the land itself; the same thing is likely to occur in ANWR if oil drilling is allowed on a large scale.

Using less oil and developing alternative sources of energy will help our economy more than further drilling for oil in Alaska will.

Americans use a lot of oil. If we used less, both individuals and the government could save money. There are several reasons why we use so much oil, but there are also many ways we can use less.

First of all, oil costs less in the United States than in most other countries, primarily because oil taxes here are much lower. For example, in 2005 a gallon of gasoline in the United States cost around $2.50, while in Europe it cost around $6.00 or more. Because oil is so expensive, Europeans are more careful about how much gas they use. If the United States government were to raise gas taxes, the government would make more money and people would learn to use less oil.

The relatively low price of our oil has meant that Americans have not always been careful about their oil use. Over the past 20 years, the speed limit on many highways in the United States has been raised. As a result, Americans use more gas than ever, because the faster a car goes, the more gas it uses. Also, sport utility vehicles (SUVs), which are much less fuel-efficient than most cars, have become very popular in the United States. If, like people in other countries, Americans drove more fuel-efficient cars or used public transportation more, we'd use less oil.

We could also save money by using less plastic, since plastic is made from oil. So many products that are wrapped in plastic don't need to be. Think about all of the plastic that packages a CD, or how about foods such as snack cakes that come in a plastic tray and are then wrapped in plastic, then boxed, then wrapped in plastic again? This is such a waste! It would be easy for us to use less plastic and, therefore, less oil, if we eliminated unnecessary packaging.

We could also help our economy by developing alternative sources of energy—which would provide new jobs for scientists, engineers, and many others. These unlimited, renewable, alternative energy sources include solar power from the sun, hydropower from water, and wind power. It has been estimated that we can get 8 to 15 times more energy from solar power than from all of the potential oil in the Arctic National Wildlife Refuge. We can also use alternative sources of energy to power our cars. Cars are being developed that use less gas or even no gas at all. Alternative fuels for cars include hydrogen-powered fuel cells and vegetable oil. If we make greater use of these vehicles and alternative fuels, we will use less crude oil. If the United States became a world leader in oil alternatives, we could make money from new technologies while using less oil and polluting less.

The United States Geological Survey (USGS) estimates that there are between 5.7 and 16 billion barrels in Area 1002 of the Arctic National Wildlife Refuge. Even the highest estimate would only increase the world oil reserves by 0.4 percent. If the oil from Area 1002 were used as the only source of oil for the United States, it would only last about 7 to 20 months. Does it make sense to harm this important habitat for such a small amount of oil?

The Solar Two Power Station in California captures sunlight with mirrored panels and converts it into energy.

Also, if oil companies were to drill in Area 1002, it would take about eight to ten years of exploration and development before oil from ANWR would actually reach American markets. That means that drilling for oil in Alaska will not fulfill our need for oil in the near future, nor will it make the United States independent from Middle East oil sources. And by the time we actually get the oil, there may be more options for alternative energies.

Many oil companies are not even interested in drilling in the Arctic because it is too costly. Oil companies must spend more money making sure that their equipment works properly and that their workers are safe in the harsh arctic climate. According to some economists, we would need to obtain at least seven billion barrels of oil to yield a profit. But given current estimates, it is not certain that we would find this much. If it is not profitable to drill for oil in Alaska, why ruin the land in order to do it?

Oil drilling can also hurt the economy. Oil spills can damage fishing areas and seriously affect the livelihood of fishermen. And fish that are contaminated with oil cannot be sent to markets and sold so the economy of the entire fishing industry could suffer from oil drilling.

Other hidden costs may result from damage to the environment. Some scientists believe that oil is a major cause of global warming. Further increases in the average temperature of the earth will cause economic problems for farmers and businesses like ski resorts. As the earth warms and the ice at the poles melts, people who live on the coasts will find their homes flooded and destroyed. All of these changes will be costly—and perhaps even deadly.

Workers clean up an oil spill in Anacortes Bay, Washington.

Conclusion

We should not drill for oil in protected areas!

You've read the reasons why I believe we should use less oil and not drill for new oil in protected areas in the United States. I hope you agree that we need to find alternative sources of energy and for raw materials for our products instead.

When I think about the future, I can imagine two possible worlds. The first—bleak and frightening—would come about if we continue to use as much oil as we do now. The countries that still had oil would control the rest of the world by setting very high prices for a barrel of oil. Some countries that couldn't afford the oil might not be able to produce the energy and products they needed. The United States, because it doesn't have enough of its own oil, would be among those countries in trouble.

The answer, however, is not to drill for more oil in protected areas. That would result in natural, protected lands being destroyed. The ground would be torn up and contaminated with oil and other chemicals. The temperature of the earth would increase as a result of global warming. Many animals and plants would die.

An oil refinery in front of the Cascade Mountains in Washington State

The other world I can imagine is much brighter; it is one in which we are smart enough to move away from our dependence on oil. We will have cut down on the amount of energy and packaging that we use. People will use trains, buses, bikes, and even their own two feet to get to school and work. Farmers will use non-oil-based pesticides and fertilizers.

In this future, people will work to create alternatives to gas-powered cars, plastics, and other oil-based products. Windmills, solar panels, and water turbines will provide renewable energy. Our economy will be strong because there will be many new jobs for people working with oil alternatives. With less dependence on oil, the land will be healthier. Energy production will not cause global warming or pollution, and we will not throw out as many plastic packages and waste products. The earth will be a cleaner, more beautiful place to live.

To me the choice is clear: We can't wait until the world is in more serious trouble as a result of oil drilling. We must use our knowledge of the problems that drilling causes to strive to make the world a better place now. We must decide to use less oil and develop alternative sources of energy.

Should We Drill for Oil in Protected Areas?